T0196459

HEAVEN SENT

HEAVEN SENT

Pamela Summerhill

authorHOUSE®

AuthorHouse™
1663 Liberty Drive
Bloomington, IN 47403
www.authorhouse.com
Phone: 1-800-839-8640

© 2012 by Pamela Summerhill. All rights reserved.

No part of this book may be reproduced, stored in a retrieval system, or transmitted by any means without the written permission of the author.

Published by AuthorHouse   10/04/2012

ISBN: 978-1-4685-9495-9 (sc)
ISBN: 978-1-4685-9494-2 (e)

Library of Congress Control Number: 2012907201

This book is printed on acid-free paper.

Because of the dynamic nature of the Internet, any web addresses or links contained in this book may have changed since publication and may no longer be valid. The views expressed in this work are solely those of the author and do not necessarily reflect the views of the publisher, and the publisher hereby disclaims any responsibility for them.

CONTENTS

ACKNOWLEDGEMENT

To my Father in Heaven
Who continues to strengthen my Heart
And mind for his Glory, I praise your Holy name
Jesus and I Love you

To my husband Jerry thank you
For your love and support through out
These 29 years I Love You
To my Children
Terrance Jehrika and Jemeka
Without you guys this couldn't have happen
I Love You

I would also like to thank my Pastor
Rev. Dr. David G. Reynolds
For allowing me to spread my talents
Through our church to spiritually enhance
The ministries there
And thank you to my church family who believed in me

To Emma Payton
Thank You for your hard work,
Knowledge Prayers and Push
I couldn't have done it without you

DEDICATION

I would like to dedicate this book to my Parents

Charles E. Neal Sr. and Willie Mae Hicks

Who stood by us as children and walked us through this life
before they departed this earth, I Love You Daddy and Mama
For the Love strength and character they built in
me and my siblings; Leona, Charles, Kenneth, Jerry,
Ruby and Ronald

HEAVENLY FATHER TOUCH

HEAVENLY FATHER AS OUR JOURNEY BEGINS;
WE THANK YOU FOR OUR BLESSINGS AGAIN AND AGAIN.
ON TAKING THIS JOURNEY YOU'VE CAPTURED OUR HEARTS;
YOU'VE MADE A WAY AND PROVIDED A START.
OUR HEARTS BURSTING WITH EXCITEMENT FOR THE
ADVENTURE WE SEEK;
LORD ALLOW US TO HAVE A MAKEOVER THAT'S TOTALLY
COMPLETE.
COMPLETE WITH OUR LOVE GRACE MERCY AND MORE;
ALLOW US TO RECEIVE AS WE ENTER THROUGH THESE
DOORS.
YOU KNEW OF THIS PLACE WHERE WE NEEDED TO COME;
A WOMENS RETREAT WHERE YOUR WORK WOULD BE DONE.
WE PRESENT OURSELVES TO YOU IN ALL SIZES SHAPES AND
COLORS;
LORD WE PRAISE YOUR NAME AS WE SHOW LOVE FOR ONE
ANOTHER.
OUR STEPS YOU'VE ORDERED FROM EAST TO WEST;
TESTED OUR FAITH AND FOUND US AT OUR BEST.

FAITH, HOPE, AND LOVE JUST TO NAME A FEW;
COME TOGETHER IN HARMONY JUST LIKE THE MORNING
  DEW.
WE STAND WITH OUR ARMS OUTSTRETCHED AND OPEN
  WIDE;
LORD TOUCH AND MAKE US OVER FROM THE INSIDE.
OUR SOULS CRY OUT FOR YOUR WISDOM WORDS;
THROUGH THE HEARTS OF OTHERS WE'VE SILENTLY
  HEARD.
WITH YOUR GUIDANCE WE CAME TO BE MADE OVER;
SUBMITTING OUR ALL FROM SHOULDER TO SHOULDER.
LIKE THE CHURCH STEEPLE KNOWN AROUND THE
  WORLD;
SHINE IN ME LORD AND MAKE ME YOUR PEARL.
DESIGNED LIKE A SYMBOL IN HONOR OF YOU;
TOGETHER WE'RE THE STRAND WHO WILL REPRESENT
  TOO.
WITH OUR HEARTS JUST FULL AND READY TO GLOW;

HOLY SPIRIT LET YOUR LIGHT SHINE SO THAT OTHERS MAY
 KNOW.
KNOW THAT I'M YOUR CHILD SOMEONE THEY CAN TRUST;
AND TO BE LIKE YOU SALVATION IS A MUST.
GOD YOU KNOW MY HEART AND WHAT IT NEEDS;
MAKE ME OVER LORD SO THAT I CAN PLANT A SEED.
ALLOW GOD TO HOLD YOU IN HIS ARMS AS YOU GLORIFY
 HIS NAME;
GO OUT AND SPREAD HIS WORD HE WILL BLESS YOU JUST
 THE SAME.
IN THE NAME OF JESUS AMEN
DEACONESS SUMMERHILL

3 SPECIALS

WHEN I THINK ABOUT MY CHILDREN AND HOW THEY'VE GROWN,
THEIR NOT LOVED ANY DIFFERENT FROM THE DAY THEY WERE BORN.
I'M GLAD I CAN SAY THAT I LOVE THEM THE SAME,
EACH ONE HAD A SPECIAL TIME WHEN THEY WERE NAMED.
WITH MY FIRST I ATE FISH AND CHOCOLATE SHAKES,
HE CAN'T STAND FISH IT MAKES HIS STOMACH ACHE.
WITH MY SECOND I ATE PIZZA DAY AND NIGHT,
SHE LOVES IT SO WELL SHE COULD EAT IT WRONG OR RIGHT.
WITH MY THIRD I ATE SQUASH WITH ONIONS AND CHEESE,
SHE SAYS SHE DOESN'T LIKE IT JUST EATS IT CAUSED I'M PLEASED.
WE BRING THEM UP IN CHURCH JESUS SAID WE SHOULD,
WE LIKE DOING THINGS THAT'S FOR THEIR OWN GOOD.
EACH BIRTHING EXPERIENCE WAS SPECIAL IN IT'S OWN WAY,

KNOT KNOWING THEIR ARRIVAL IS SUPRISING I MUST SAY.
BIRTHMARKS ARE SPECIAL A CONNECTION SOMEHOW,
IT SHOWS US HOW 9 MONTHS CAN MAKE YOU GO WOW.
SPECIAL TO ME SPECIAL TO YOU,
ONLY MOMS KNOW THE CONNECTION OF THE TWO.
WHETHER ONE AT A TIME OR TWO TO THREE,
THE BOND IS THERE YOU WOULD HAVE TO BE THERE TO SEE.
OH THE PAIN THE PAIN IT TAKES YOUR ALL,
WHEN IT HIT YOU WHAT NAME DID YOU CALL?
EACH ONE DIFFERENT IN IT'S OWN WAY,
SOME HARSH SOME QUICK SOME JUST STAY.
TIME TIME HOURS WELL SPENT
MINUTES MINUTES OH HOW THEY WENT.
THEN IT WAS OVER THE CHILD WAS BORN
JUST LIKE THEY SAY IT'S QUIET BEFORE THE STORM.
3-SPECIAL BABIES BORN IN THREE DIFFERENT PLACES,
ALL THE SAME PAIN WITH THEIR BEAUTIFUL FACES.
1 BOY 2 GIRLS CHILDREN GALORE,
I LOVE THEM ALL JUST DON'T WANT ANYMORE.
                              PAMELA SUMMERHILL

"A LOVE THAT BINDS"

* Circle of rings that ties us together
   A binding of Love that last forever
* Circle of rings diamonds and things treasures and stones
   Never having to be alone
* New love, young love season and all
   What God binds together it's on him you can call
* Like a slow dance of love you look into her eyes
   The love you have for him is of no surprise
* Look what God has created in each one of us
   His power of love a bond a trust
* He gave us the keys to unlock each others hearts
   Binding us together that's just one part
* Look at her isn't she sweet
   God gave her to you she's yours to keep
* Like rubber bands elastic and glue
   Nothing is stronger than the love of two
* No one knows the love two people share
   It flows differently in each and every pair

* God gave us love for each other so deep
   We hold it in our soul its ours to keep
* Like that telepathy you have from being together so long
   You know each others thoughts like humming a song
* Vows are shared love overflowing
   God in us he sees us glowing
* A special evening with dinner and candle light
   Setting the mood for romance to be right
A Love That Binds

A MESSENGER

Hear Ye Hear ye a message so clear,
Sent from above for your listening ear.
Take a look around so you can see,
The Love ones who belong in your family tree.
Our lifeline flowing but not in our veins,
Flourishing and flowing in Jesus name.
Together we gather with love overflowing,
Fathers and Mothers our children still growing.
Hear this message for its plain and clear,
It is for all our families to hear.
One by one we are born again,
For our God is the one who keeps us from sin.
Every Man Woman Boy or Girl,
Get up close get personal as he blesses our world.
For the entrance to your heart you hold the key,
Let God come in so you will see.
It's his schedule we should follow,
Without his leadership our lives would be hollow.
As you were trained up as a child,

A born again Christian became your very own style.
Guided by Gods grace mercy and love,
Into your heart like peace from above.
The tools he shares and those who choose to hear it,
Beatitudes Commandments and Fruits of the Spirit.
Sixty six books all in order,
The word alive like living water.
Then the word of God travels through your life,
Boys Girls Husbands Wives.
Love and Laughter from God is real,
Oh the Joy, the Peace He teaches you can feel.
This is your family this is the tree,
A part of your life your History.
Amen

A SEASON FOR LOVE

Sweet Love, In Giving God Thanks This Season For The Joy We
Bring Each Other;
By His Grace And His Mercy We Continue To Cherish One Another.
Looking Back To Each And Every Year;
We Cherish The Moments We Hold So Dear.
As We Reflect Back On This Season Of Love;
We Thank God For This Union Created From Above.
Like Salt And Pepper Day And Night;
Gods Earth Is Seasoned For Our Own Delight.
Winter Spring Summer And Fall;
He Gives Us These Seasons To Comfort Us All.
We Come Together For A Feast;
For The Love Of Family And Closeness We Keep.
Sharing The Warmth Of A Cozy Lit Fire On A Cold Winters Night;
Let The Fruits Of The Spirit Be Set In Your Sight.
What Season Of Marriage Do We Share;
This Is Our_____Thanksgiving As A Pair.
Lord We Thank You For Another Season Of Solemn Strength;
And For The Beatitudes You So Gracefully Sent.
Blessed By Your Spirit Amen

AMAZING DANCE

TODAY I WATCHED YOU DANCE FACE TO FACE
ONE WITH POWER ONE WITH GRACE
THE BEAUTY OF MOVEMENT GOD IN IT
GLORY TO HIS NAME AND HEAVEN SENT
DRESSED IN WHITE PURE IN HEART
ALL ABOUT HIM A GOOD PLACE TO START
YOU HAVE ALLOWED GOD TO USE YOU AT SUCH
   A YOUNG AGE
GIFTED TO DANCE WITH POWER AND PRAISE
TEARS OF JOY ROLL DOWN OUR FACE
MINISTERING IN DANCE YOU COULD BE OTHER PLACES
TWIRLING SWIRLING JESUS IN OUR MIST
SPIRIT FLOWING LIKE THE WORDS ON THE DISK
I THANK YOU BOTH STRONG AND LOUD
FOR DOING GODS WORK YOU HAVE MADE US VERY PROUD
          DEACONESS SUMMERHILL

ANGEL OF THE NIGHT

You came to me in the mid of night
The comfort you bought was just right
It was a year ago next week
You bought me something I could keep
But I didn't realize how much it meant
Until I saw a friends face after you were sent
I realize now that you're an angel of the night
You deliver your blessings when the time is right
Barely awake weary with pain
I did not know what joy would bring
I saw how much love comfort and care
The bear provided with each little hair
Oh the memory came back of that one night
How you came in and out what a beautiful sight
You fluffed my pillows and straightened my sheets
You asked the nurse about my drink and eats
I was in such pain no comfort in sight
Until you left my blessing; I hugged it all night
When Miriam told me she held on tight
To her angel bear all through the night
I remembered the softness against my face

I felt when you came it was by God's grace
When I saw the peace upon her face
I remembered the night in that lonely place
And how you came by to comfort me
I saw what she felt I was able to see
So Angel of the night, keep us in your heart
Let your light shine it plays a big part
A part in our lives that helps us to remember
Remember the night the night you delivered

Jacque thanks for the Memory
Deaconess Summerhill

ANOINTED VOICES

It was the anointing of your voice that pierced my soul
That song of Zion a sweet story told.
The Blessed notes that rang in my ears
Voices so strong my heart had tears.
Praising his name in high notes and low
The lifting of souls and voices galore.

COMFORT MY HEART

We sit we wait we cry we wonder,
Why our children are being killed out yonder
Oh God why does it happen so frequently today,
Why oh why is it happening this way
They are all babies harmless and pure
Helpless terrified and scared I'm sure,
Why the children so young so small
Help help please hear our call
Teach them keep them safe and sound
Love them hug them Watch them year around

CONNECTED

*Father I know that with you in my heart I have a life line to
Salvation
And as I accept this honor through you I have been blessed with
grace and mercy.*

*The wonders of others look upon us
They don't seem to know it is in you we trust
Having that connection to you is an honor
Sharing your word just being a donor
Depositing your word into others
Shinning that light into our sisters and brothers
Connected to you connected to me,
It's the word of God whom we want them to see*

CRUSADERS

At the ages of 6-11
The children learn all about heaven
Each time that we come together
We will discuss more than the weather
Young minds to study Gods word
And bring good news of what they've heard
Sharing caring and loving to learn
All Gods children have great concern
Concern about their future ready willing and able
Bringing Gods blessings to his glorious table

DEAR GOD

Today at church I let out a cry
I didn't know how, I didn't know why
The Minister was talking and she looked my way
Tears started building in my eyes right away
I tried to stop them from flowing as quickly as I could
But they only came faster, now I understood
God you said let go and let your tears flow
For I know what I'm doing to help you to grow
Grow in my spirit dear child of mine
It doesn't happen all at once it will take some time
Tears of joy pain and laughter
A river could form if they came any faster
A circle of Angels we all gathered around
Tears still flowing some lay to the ground
Angels laying low some standing tall
The spirit moving amongst us all

DID YOU KNOW?

You took my kindness for weakness God gave me that
And you don't even know him so you have to give it back.
My best friends name is Jesus I tell him everything
So when you mess with me you're going up against the King.
We pray we sing we laugh we cry
If you know him like I do you will be on his side.
Jesus is my Savior and he can be yours too
John 3:16 tells you what he Sacrificed for you.
Glory to God the Highest King
He left those 66 books to explain everything.
They come together in one complete set
So start at the beginning you will not regret
That's LOVE

DREAMS UNTOLD

I saw his power
I saw his grace
There was an anointing all over the place

He in me
I in the word
Sun in Son
Obedience heard

We honor his spirit
We honor his might
Surrounding our hearts
And ready to take flight

We have the history
Of his story you see
Life everlasting sealed
Within me

FOREVER FRIENDS

PEOPLE COME AND PEOPLE GO
IN AND OUT OF OUR LIVES WE KNOW
BUT THEN THERE'S GOD WHO IS FOREVER
HE BRINGS US FRIENDS FOREVER AND EVER
EVERLASTING HE'S OUR FRIEND
WE KNOW HIM WE LOVE HIM TO THE END
HE IS ONE FRIEND WHO IS FOREVER
HE WILL NEVER LEAVE US NO NOT EVER
HOW LONG IS FOREVER

. . . .

IT DOESN'T STOP THERE IS NO END
DO YOU KNOW HIM AS YOUR FOREVER FRIEND
GOD IS FOREVER NO NOT NEVER
HE'S THERE FOR US NO MATTER WHAT EVER
FOREVER IS EVER, EVER AND EVER
FROM BEGINNING TO END GOD WILL BE YOUR FOREVER
    FRIEND

. . . .

GOD IS FOREVER THE FRIEND WE NEED
HE'LL NEVER TURN HIS BACK EVEN WHEN WE SUCCEED
FRIENDS FOREVER HIS LOVE IS SO TRUE
MUSTARD SEED FAITH IS ALL HE ASK OF YOU
FOREVER, HOW LONG FOREVER IS WHEN
GOD WILL BE YOUR FOREVER FRIEND
FOREVER FOREVER FOREVER FRIENDS

. . . .

MY HEART IN HIS HANDS
MY HEART CAN SEE THE GOODNESS I FEEL
HOW I CARRY HIS NAME FROM MY HEAD TO MY HEEL
MY WALK MY TALK MY HEART YOU SEE
GOD TOOK ME IN HIS HANDS FOR ETERNITY
NOW THAT'S FOREVER

. . . .

LOVE PAMELA

GOD'S PLAN

The glory He gives allowing us to pray
Our prayers answered in his loving way
Lord, Lord we glorify your name
Our love for you will never change
We know of your grace we pray for your mercy

GUIDED IN HIS WORD

WHAT WILL KEEP YOU FROM WALKING THOSE STREETS
OF GOLD,
THE DOORS TO HEAVEN ARE OPEN THERS'S NO SIGN
SAYING CLOSED
YOU'VE WALKED WITH HIM AND TALKED WITH HIM HE'S
KEPT YOU UP LATE,
YOU'VE HEARD HIM TALK OF THOSE PEARLIE GATES
THERE ARE CERTAIN THINGS THAT WILL GET YOU OFF
TRACK'
BUT YOU CAN REST ASSURED KNOWING THE TRINITY
HAS YOUR BACK
GOD WILL TAKE US THROUGH STORMS BECAUSE THEY
MAKE US STRONGER,
THEN AFTER OUR TESTIMONY'S WE DON'T SUFFER ANY
LONGER
STAND STRONG FOR HE'S THE SOURCE OF OUR
STRENGTH,
AND WITH HIS HIGH STANDARDS THERE'S NO GREATER
LENGTH
AS YOU PRAISE GOD FOR THE WORD,
DON'T TRY TO CLOUD WHAT YOUR EARS HAVE HEARD
WHEN YOU FALL ON YOUR KNEES TO PRAY,
CRY OUT TO GOD TO SHED SOME LIGHT TO YOUR DAY
HIGHER IN GLORY HIGHER IN GRACE,

KEEP REACHING KEEP TEACHING KEEP SEEKING HIS
   FACE
HELP LET'S BRING SOULS TO CHRIST,
HE'LL GIVE YOU SALVATION FOR THE REST OF YOUR
   LIFE
IN YOUR KINGDOM STEPS HE REVEALS A REVELATION,
THEN YOU TURN AROUND AND PRAISE HIM FOR THAT
   SWEET CONFORMATION
HALLELUJAH TO GOD IN JESUS NAME AMEN
               DEACONESS SUMMERHILL

HE CARES

We can count on one hand the things we have done
The challenge would be to name them one by one
Things will happen through out your life
And some we encounter will take us through strife
We must hold on to the word of God
And overcome the obstacles that may seem hard
Protection and guidance comes from above
Seek him daily let him shower you with his love
Let him ride on the tail of your coat
Mustard seed faith will cause you to gloat
His amazing awesome and abundant grace
Will capture your heart and glow on your face
That's when the shinning he has will come through
And the light of Christ will be upon you
Glory Glory Hallelujah
Living for God is the righteous thing to do
He has a path that is easy to follow
Your mind body and soul won't be hollow

The kingdom of God is where you're headed
Take in his word let it become imbedded
A journey seeker is who you should be
He gives us his word to study you see
He'll cleanse you of all your doubts
So give him the chance to help you out
Out of darkness and into the light
His amazing grace he'll give you with all his might

Amen

HIS LOVE

THE MOMENT YOU FEEL THE SPIRIT OF GOD
YOUR HEART BURSTING WITH LOVE
THE TWINKLING OF STARS GLOWING SO BRIGHT
SHINNING SO CLEAR LIKE GUIDING LIGHTS
AT THIS SPECIAL TIME OF THE YEAR
THE WONDERFUL LOVE OF FAMILY SO DEAR
OH THAT LOVE THAT DEEPLY FILLS THE AIR
WITH THAT PERFECT GIF T YOU WANT TO SHARE
COLORS ON COLORS SO BIG AND BOLD
SPARKLES OF RED BLUE GREEN SILVER AND GOLD
OUR FATHER THE CREATOR SO UNIQUELY BORN
YOUR FIRST GIFT OF ALL IS TO AWAKE ON CHRISTMAS MORN
HIS LOVE HIS LIGHT CAN BE A REFLECTION IN YOU
A GIANT STEP, GO OUT ON A LIMB FOR ALL YOU DO

BIG LOVE

HE'LL MAGNIFY YOUR SPIRIT AS YOU TRUST IN HIS
NAME
ONCE YOU BOW TO HIM YOU'LL NEVER BE THE SAME
LOOK AT YOUR SISTER SITTING NEXT TO YOU
SHOW HER LOVE AS SOMEONE SHOWED YOU
SHOW HER LOVE LIFT HER UP
TELL HER OF HIS GOODNESS HOW FULL IS HER CUP
UNIQUENESS HE GIVES FOREVER HE LIVES
SURROUND YOUR HEART WITH HIS LOVE
LOOK UP MY SISTERS YOUR HEART HAS FULLNESS
THIS ROOM IS FILLED WITH LOVE
ALMIGHTY THAT'S LOVE
OMNIPOTENT THAT'S LOVE
CREATOR THAT'S LOVE
JEHOVAH JIRAH THAT'S LOVE
ALPHA AND OMEGA THAT'S LOVE
IN JESUS NAME AMEN
DEACONESS SUMMERHILL

KNOWING HIM

God knows our weakness
God knows our strength
We have to stand strong no matter the length
Let him hold you into the night
He will give you comfort just right
We have to love and honor him through and through
And ask him for forgiveness for all that we do
Seen and unseen known and unknown
He's worth all the glory his mercy has shown
Our blessings we know are the ones we have shared
The ones full of love for those we have cared.
God Bless Our Souls

LIFE

How do you hate the people you love?
If you feel that bad you should seek God above.
Growing up with rules in life,
It's very hard when your young and full of strife.
Just when you think your problems are big,
There's another person out there whose worries are beyond big.
You can't go around with hate in your heart,
God won't allow it or he won't take part.
He won't take a part in your hateful thoughts,
So just let go and don't get caught.
Caught with these thoughts of hate in your mind,
Repentance is good, not evil just kind.
While growing up life can be cruel,
A child doesn't understand follow the rule.
The rules of life may not seem good,
It's not easy for parents like they think it should.

It's hard it's harsh but we all have to go through,
Some our fault and theirs too.
When your older you might understand,
The disciplined I've learned came from my mother's hand.
So all that hatred you have in your heart,
You need to let go of the devil's part.
As parents we hurt the same way you do,
We would never ever let anything happen to you.
So open up your heart and learn to forgive,
Because Jesus gave us his all for us to live.
Go live your life and follow your dreams,
Stop feeling sorry life is like a stream.

LOVE IN THE SEASON

Marriage Enrichment
Gleam in your eyes,
The sound of your cries.
Silent murmurs of love so deep,
The whispers of Love the passion you seek.
Love drifting through the air,
Giving thanks for the beauty we share.
The flavor you bring into my life,
The seasonings of Love and holiday spice.
The Holiday season and the Love it brings,
The laughter of family, the joy in the songs they sing.
Togetherness food family and friends,
The Grace of God and the Love he sends.
The seasons come and then they go,
Year by year your love continues to grow.
It's that cozy cold weather,
That will surly draw you together.

Pamela Summerhill

The newness of spring,
A lovely song to sing.
Hot summers and ocean waves,
Laughter of love that time saves.
Leaves falling fresh and crisp,
Holding touching longing for a kiss.
God's creation year around Love,
So Gracefully sent from above.

LOVE TO YOU AND I

LOOK AT THE CONNECTION AND HOW IT CAME TO BE
HE IN YOUR LIFE AND GOD IN THE LEAD
GOD KNEW IT WOULD TAKE TWO HEARTS TO LOVE
YOU WERE HER HALF SENT FROM ABOVE
LOCKED AND SEALED LOVED AND DESIRED
GOD SECURED TWO HEARTS ON FIRER
WE HONOR GOD FOR THE SELECTION OF HIS CHOICE
HE LINKED US TOGETHER TO HAVE ONE VOICE
HE SUPPLIED US WOMEN WITH BEAUTY AND GRACE
THE MEN WITH POWER AND STRENGTH THAT SHOWS IN
*   HIS FACE*
EVEN OUR HANDS OUR WALK OUR POSE
WE CAN TRULY SAY GOD GAVE US THOSE
THE TALLNESS IN YOUR WALK THE BONE IN YOUR BACK
THE CAGE OF YOUR RIBS GOD DID ALL THAT
THE EXPRESSIONS OF LOVE YOU SO OFTEN SHARE
GUIDED BY GOD TO SHOW HER YOU CARE

Pamela Summerhill

IT'S THAT HANDSOME LOOK YOU HAVE ON YOUR FACE
WHEN YOU SAY SHE'S BEAUTIFUL AND NOTHINGS OUT
  OF PLACE
YOUR SILENT WHISPERS THAT FILL HER EARS
OR THE SILENCE YOU SEE IN HER TEARS
A LOVE OH LOVE WITH STRENGTH SO STRONG
A CONCLUSION FROM GOD WHEN NOTHING IS WRONG
LOVE IS LOVE IS LOVE SO NEW AND OLD
YOUNG AND LONG AND BLESSES OUR SOUL.   AMEN

LOVES CREATION

It is him who shows us the Love we must have
A feeling of strength with the blood he shed
So bright so pure and dripping from his head,
He gave us love when he suffered and died
Just hearing his story brought tears to my eyes,
These are your sisters tell them how you feel
Share with her how your God is real,
Lift her up let her know you are there
Look in her face tell her you care,
We are the women God has chosen here
We are the women that have no fear,
Standing strong in his holy name
Letting us know it's for us he came,
You look at your ribs and I look at mine
We give God the credit for his creative design,
With our arms locked and standing in the gap
This is the Love I'm talking about,

God would be pleased if he saw us now
We strengthen our Faith and he shows us how,
A life of Love for our sisters in Christ
It's for Gods love we make this sacrifice,
We give birth to this earth
God chose us he knows our worth,
Our love for family friends and others
He created us to be awesome Mothers.

Father I Thank You for These Words of Wisdom to
Share with Women of God

LOVING THEM

Whose baby is this that I hold so near
And what is the name of his real Madear,
I've raised a many across this earth
Like a surrogate Mother waiting for the birth,
Many years have swiftly gone by
As they leave it's so hard not to cry,
You hold their issues in the palms of your hands
It's not just here it's across the land,
The love comfort and the support we give
Is a lasting memory of the life they've lived,
Love hugs kisses and all
Tears tears oh how they do fall,
We are the people who comfort them well
And listen while there's a story to tell,
We confidently hold onto their lives
Whether it be siblings husbands or wives,

To love is easy and the security they need
That's why we treat them like our very own seed,
Not just a teacher but much much more
Loving caring and listening for shore,
Believe it or not out of all that I've raised
Each one different in their very own ways,
I pray to God that they be protected
Their thoughts their dreams of anything rejected,
I know he is the one who keeps them safe
And guides our hearts with amazing grace,
Softly tenderly lovingly working
Together with Jesus from the moment of burping.

MOVING ONWARD

Another year has come and gone,
Your strength in God has allowed you to carry on.
Walking through life with Jesus by your side,
A daily journey and stepping high with pride.
The love of memories that run real deep,
In your thoughts, in your heart, their yours to keep.
In your life you hold a lot of history,
Your love your life it's longevity.
A walk in your shoes is special to us,
Wisdom understanding training a must.
We thank God for the time you give,
Teaching about life and how to live.
In your God given days you've told your story,
How he bought you through and you gave him the Glory.
Memories like Blessings are shared all the time,

Those are the things that help you to shine.
We thank you for leading this generation,
We are very proud that in God you have relations.
You too were once a child,
Trained up in Jesus style.
With Boldness and beauty Strength and courage,
You passed on the knowledge of wisdom in storage.
You've come to a time where your worries are few
Trusting in God for all that you do.
Amen

MY BLESSINGS

Their voices rang out and pierced my soul
The African children not many years old
My heart so full my beats rang out
The tears on my face the sign of a shout
They lifted us up they fed our souls
The love they spread was like heated coals
Full of joy laughter hugs and more
Praises in song dances galore
I will never forget the look on their faces
After their performance as they returned to their places
My blessings came song after song and dance after dance
The children wowed us with an awesome stance

OF GOLDEN YEARS

THERE'S A LOT YOU'VE CONQUERED THROUGH OUT YOUR LIVES,
HE YOUR HUSBAND SHE YOUR WIFE.
I DO AND I DO ARE NOT JUST TWO WORDS'
THEY COME FROM ABOVE GOD TRULY HEARD.
FIFTY YEARS IS QUITE A LONG TIME,
YOU'VE LAUGHED YOU'VE LOVED YOU'VE DANCED AND DINED.
YOU'VE PRAYED YOU CRIED AND SAW MANY YEARS PAST,
BUT WITHOUT EACH OTHER YOUR LOVE COULDN'T LAST.
YOU JUST DIDN'T COME INTO EACH OTHERS LIFE,
WITH THE LORDS BLESSING YOU BECAME HUSBAND AND WIFE.
YOU SEE THE LORD LOVES IT WHEN HIS PLAN COMES TOGETHER,
SOFT AND GENTLE LIKE THE WHISPER OF A FEATHER.
GOD KNEW YOU TWO SHOULD BE TOGETHER,
THROUGH STORMS PAIN BIRTH OR WHAT EVER.

THE THINGS YOU'VE DONE HAVE BOUGHT YOU A LONG WAY,
THE LORDS LOVE PEACE AND JOY HAS HELPED YOU TO STAY.
STAY TOGETHER THROUGH THICK AND THIN,
TOGETHER FOREVER IT COMES FROM WITH IN.
HE YOUR CRUTCH SHE YOUR CANE,
THE YEARS THE YEARS NONE ARE THE SAME.
MEMORIES MEMORIES OF WHAT YOU'VE DONE,
JUST THINK BACK FROM WHERE YOU'VE COME.
SO KEEP ON SHINNING AND HOLD ONTO THE KEY,
THAT GOD WILL ALLOW YOU TO SEE.
LOVE PAMELA

RUNNING FOR CHRIST

These are the children I'm talking about;
These are the children in whom we had no doubt.
We've trained them up so they'd be strong;
For in this world they will carry on.
On to the legacy of running this world;
In God's order as it continues to twirl.
The expectations of them being in charge;
To carry on as the numbers get large.
The Bible says train up a child in the way he should go;
So when he comes back he'll already know.
Know the Word of God unspoken;
As he stands to be that token.
Honoring and moving others toward the light;
The light in him held by Christ.
Christ our King He reigns supreme
He holds 66 books and says what they mean.
So when you see these children and their going all out;
Just know that it's Jesus for whom they shout.
Amen for our children

SEASONED SAINTS

Seasoned you are flavorful and unique
Your wisdom words is what others seek
It's your generation we look up too
When ever in doubt and we don't know what to do
With eyes wide open and focused on God
The challenges of life didn't seem too hard
The fruits of the spirit are the seasonings in my mind
Galations 5: 22 they come right on time
Your journey has been a well walked path unknown
And along the way it's the Beatitudes you've shown
It's you whom we hold in our hearts so dear
And taught us we have nothing to fear
Your generation our parents spoke of
Your wisdom your knowledge passed down in love
It's been such an honor to have you in our lives
From the children, teens, young men, and women husbands and wives
Connected we are and connected we'll be
By the grace of God and his devine serenity
Deaconess Pamela Summerhill

STAINED GLASS WINDOWS

I was sitting in the pews one Monday night
Looking out the windows on the left and the right,
I saw three crosses and I knew what they meant
Father Son and Holy Ghost Heaven Sent,
The stained glass window had a beautiful design
As we looked across the church oh it was Heaven devine,
The creative work was so elegantly done
The designers knew our hearts would be won,
I knew God was pleased with this order
It would serve as a purpose for every Son and Daughter,
So when you see the stained glass windows on the left and the right
Know that those three crosses were created in Gods sight.

TEACHERS OF GOOD THINGS

From Genesis to Psalms and Psalms to Revelation
The Godly things taught has kept us in relation
Relation to God and his holy word
Instilled in our hearts we've silently heard
With guidance you lead us prepare and teach us
Together teaching a journey of learning and thus
Shepherds chosen by our Lord and Savior above
Saints come teaching with the abundance of love
Sermons seminars, council and all
You've taught us how to sustain any fall
Leading and guiding hearts of heavy burdens
Mind meditation on Jesus for certain
Strong in heart from the pulpit to the pews
Delivering whispered knowledge and Holy Ghost news
The two of you together on one accord
Presenting the word for Christ our Lord
Teaching Preaching Baptizing in Jesus name
Good things taught and the vision the same
And our shepherds work continues on
Guided in glory until we're called home Amen

THANK YOU

Father I thank you today
For you sent me a hug in your own special way,
I had no idea I didn't see it coming
So strong and loving as a humming bird humming,
I feel peace in my heart with a spirit soft and calm
And remembering your word in the 23rd Psalm,
As I sit here in the pew thanking you
I pray your anointing will cover all I do,
I thank you for having me as a chosen one
I will honor your favor to be like your only begotten son,
I'm trying to hold up trying not to cry
I know your love is strong enough to last until I die,
My hope my faith my strength my courage
To keep you close these things I keep in storage,
In my heart I keep them safe and hold them dear
So when their shared I keep them near

THE BIRTH

DO YOU REMEMBER THE FIRST TIME YOU HEARD
THE STORY OF JESUS HIS BIRTH THE WORD
OPEN YOUR MIND AND TRY TO THINK BACK
HOW YOU FOUND OUT HOW DID YOU REACT
IT WAS SUCH A VERY EXCITING STORY
DOWN THROUGH THE GENERATIONS TOLD WITH GLORY
A KING WILL BE BORN TO SAVE OUR SOULS
AND IT DOSEN'T MATTER IF WERE YOUNG OR OLD
IN OUR HEARTS IS WHERE WE RECEIVE
AND ALL WE HAVE TO DO IS BELIEVE
BELIEVE HE CAME TO DIE FOR OUR SINS
RECEIVE IT BELIEVE IT AND NEW LIFE BEGINS
THEY WERE TURNED AWAY FROM ONE PLACE TO
    ANOTHER
NO ROOM IN THE INN FOR FATHER OR MOTHER
SO GOD MADE A WAY ON THIS SILENT NIGHT
TO BE BORN IN A MANGER BY THE STAR AND IT'S LIGHT
BORN UNDER A STAR ON A VERY CLEAR NIGHT

*IT WAS HIS FATHER IN HEAVEN WHO PROVIDED THE
    LIGHT
THERE HE LAY IN A MANGER SO DEAR
MARY JOSEPH AND THE SHEPHERD BOY NEAR
THE KINGS ALL TRAVELED THEY FOLLOWED THE STAR
THEY KNEW THE JOURNEY TO OUR SAVIOR WOULD BE
    FAR
A TIME FOR CELEBRATION A KING IS BORN
REJOICE REJOICE O SOUND THE HORN
HE BECAME OUR BLESSING AND SAVED US ALL
WE SHOULD THANK HIM WITH OUR PRAYERS BIG AND
    SMALL
OUR KING STILL REIGNS IN HEAVEN AND EARTH
AND THE STORY WILL NEVER CHANGE ABOUT THE NEWS
    OF HIS BIRTII*

THE JESUS I KNOW

*THE JESUS I KNOW DIED UPON THE CROSS;
HE CAME TO THIS WORLD BECAUSE THE PEOPLE WERE
LOST.
*THE JESUS I KNOW WAS BORN IN A MANGER;
THE PEOPLE HE SAVED WERE SO FULL OF ANGER.
*THE JESUS I KNOW PERFORMED MANY MIRACLES ON
EARTH;
HE LET THE PEOPLE KNOW THEIR LIVES HAD WORTH.
*THE JESUS I KNOW SUFFERED FOR US;
SO TO BE SAVED IN THIS WORLD IS A MUST.
*DO YOU KNOW THIS JESUS THAT I'M TALKING ABOUT?
TO KNOW HIM IS TO LOVE HIM WITHOUT A DOUBT.
*YOU HEAR HIS NAME ALL AROUND;
YOUR JESUS MY JESUS SOME PEOPLE PUT HIM DOWN.
*THE JESUS I KNOW HE DIED FOR YOU AND ME;
AND WHEN HE SAVES YOUR SOUL IT'S FOR ETERNITY.
*THE JESUS I KNOW WOULD YOU LIKE TO KNOW HIM
TOO?
BECAUSE SALVATION IS FREE ESPECIALLY FOR ME
AND YOU.*

SOME PEOPLE SAY THEY DON'T KNOW WHERE TO START;
IT'S ALL ABOUT YOUR MIND AND OPENING UP YOUR HEART.
OPEN UP YOUR HEART AND LET HIM COME IN;
JOHN 3:16 IS A GOOD PLACE TO BEGIN.
THE JESUS I KNOW DOESN'T STAY IN ONE PLACE;
HE'S ALL OVER THE WORLD WITH HIS AMAZING GRACE.
SO WHEN YOU LET HIM COME INTO YOUR HEART;
LET HIM KNOW THAT YOU WANT TO BE A PART;
A PART OF HIS PLAN, SALVATION, BAPTISM, PRAYER AND ALL
HE'LL ANSWER YOUR PRAYERS SO HEAR HIM CALL.

THAT'S THE JESUS I KNOW
DEACONESS SUMMERHILL

THE JOURNEY

Father Thank You
Our fellowship will be stronger in honor of you
As we change our walk to represent too
Wanting to be stronger in your word and dedicated to the scriptures
we've heard
Lord strengthen our faith by the knowledge we've gained
We give you all the glory and honor as we call out your name
Feel his touch of grace and mercy the comfort of his love
The power of his spirit that comes from above
Like the beauty of the sun that shines from the sky
When he decorated wth stars and hung them high
Seek and praise him to start your day
Remembering to honor him as you pray
Let our father take control of your life
For on his team you will have to fight
Let us not entertain the devil
Lift up your head don't stoop to his level
A child of God is the honor you hold
Let your light shine and his story be told
Your mind be filled with his words of grace

Pour your heart out to others who yearn for a place
A place in this life where our fathers light is shown
In the highest of the heavens in places unknown
To be taught and to teach but not to keep
Use the word and let God speak
He has given us gifts one by one
Salvation baptism the trinity as one
He loves us dearly so grab a hold and see
His birth his death the resurrection another three
To love him is to know him come get on board
To make this change and get on one accord
Feel now the blessings that have changed your lives
Given by God for you to survive
Father hold us as you mold us
Claim us as you change us
Teach us to walk in the presence of you
We know we'll be blessed as you guide us through
Adventurous journeys seeking a higher sight
A change in our faith to reach new heights

The feel of his strength dwelling in our hearts
Walking in newness and taking a part
In his designed plan which we have received
After claiming our savior you'll never leave
As you take your walk hold your head high
Be proud to represent your master on high

WALKING WORTHY IN YOUR CALLING

ARE WE WALKING WORTHY IN OUR CALLING?

WILL YOU WEAR THAT CROWN OF THORNS THAT JESUS WORE FOR US?

OR ARE YOU TOO WORRIED ABOUT WHAT WOULD HAPPEN TO YOUR HEAD?

WHAT WOULD BE ON YOUR MIND FIRST?

THE POINTS! WILL IT HURT WHEN IT'S BEING PUSHED DOWN ON YOUR HEAD?

OR WOULD IT BOTHER YOU THAT THE PUNCTURE WOUND WOULD CAUSE

BLOOD TO RUN DOWN YOUR FACE AND INTO YOUR EYES.

WOULD YOU BE WORTHY OF HAVING THE NAILS PUSHED INTO YOUR HANDS AND FEET?

THE JOURNEY BEGAN WITH THE DEATH.

WHAT EVER YOUR CALLING MAYBE,

THERE SHOULDN'T BE ANY REASON WHY YOU WOULD EXCUSE YOURSELF, FROM DOING THE WORK OF OUR LORD AND SAVIOR.

HIS MERCY ENDURETH FOREVER

WE ARE ALL GODS CHILDREN OBEDIENCE COMES WITH
 HONOR.
AS HIS CHILDREN OUR LORD EXPECTS US TO OBEY HIM.
WE ARE LIKE THE FRUITS OF THE SPIRIT, LIKE GODS
 CHILDREN WITH THEIR OWN PERSONALITY
WHICH OF THESE FRUITS BEST DESCRIBES YOU
LOVE—ARE YOU GIVING IT
JOY-ARE YOU SHOWING IT
PEACE—DO YOU HAVE IT
PATIENCE-GOT TO HAVE IT
KINDNESS—HAS TO BE SHOWN
GOODNESS—IS IT THERE
FAITHFULNESS-ARE YOUR STEPS ORDERED
GENTLENESS—CAN IT BE SEEN IN YOU
SELF CONTROL—ARE YOU MAINTAINING IT
<u>HALLELUJAH TO THE KING</u>

WHISPERS

Last nights dream was so very real
Everything moving nothing stood still
Raging clouds falling stars
Not a sound only one car
A1957 blue Malibu is how it began
The voice of God entered in
His words were soft He said "Here I Am"
He blew softly a quiet wind without any sound
We fell easily down to the ground
As we breathe in his breath that was so deliciously good
A taste of his love as sweet as we thought it would.

(The Bible Says He Will Never Leave nor Forsake You)

YOU KEEP ME

Father my love for you makes me teary eyed
On this thankful morning I really cried
Thinking of how you care for my soul
A precious jewel a sparkle you make me whole
The spoken word to strengthen my life
The armor of God to keep me from strife
You give me love grace mercy and hope
So my life with you will not slope
Lifted higher in my daily walk
You provide your peace for a clearer thought
I cherish all the glory you provide
Your prayer your love your faith it's inside
Inside of me I hold all so dear
Your life your strength I keep it all near
My mind is made up about you being in control
Your Son shinning in me as I stand real bold
I belong to you and proud to let others know
It's you who makes the difference it's not about a show

YOUR CUP

Father I thank you for the fullness of my cup
As it tipped over you were there when grace fell out,
It was your love that kept me from doubt.
And when I spilt from it,
You were the one that kept mercy flowing,
And Love to continue growing.
So when it chipped,
It was your humbleness that caused me to keep my grip.
When it was cracked,
It was my trust in you that had my back.
The drop was the hope you gave,
In knowing I was saved.
Broken was the faith in you that held me together,
Storm by storm in any kind of weather.
Our cup is filled a little at a time,
One by one the battles come in all kinds.

Pouring and filling and filling and pouring,
With honor and strength Gods power adoring.
Sipping tasting cooling steaming,
Swirling twirling stirring cleaning.
Washed rinsed scrubbed dried,
Squeeking shinning smooth with pride.
So the fullness of my cup that brought me through,
Was Guided by God and honoring him too.
                    Deaconess Summerhill

INVITATION TO SALVATION

Romans 10:9-10

9 That if thou shalt confess with thou mouth the Lord Jesus, and shalt believe in thine heart that God hath raised him from the dead, thou shalt be saved. 10 For with the heart man believeth unto righteousness; and with the mouth confession is made unto salvation